It's Raining Cats and Dogs

By Jackie Franza
Illustrations by Steve Gray

BOWTIE
P R E S S®

A Division of BowTie, Inc.
Irvine, California

Karla Austin, *Business Operations Manager*
Nick Clemente, *Special Consultant*
Kendra Strey, *Project Editor*
Jill Dupont, *Production*
Cover and layout design by Janet Moir McCaffrey

Library of Congress Cataloging-in-Publication Data

Franza, Jackie.
   It's raining cats and dogs : making sense of animal phrases / by Jackie Franza ; illustrations by Steve Gray.
     p. cm.
   ISBN 1-931993-74-2
   1. English language—Etymology. 2. English language—Terms and phrases. 3. Animals—Nomenclature (Popular) 4. Animals—Terminology. 5. Animals—Folklore. 6. Figures of speech. I. Gray, Steve, 1950– II. Title.

   PE1583.F66 2006
   422—dc22
                2005020106

BowTie Press®
A Division of BowTie, Inc.
3 Burroughs
Irvine, CA 92618

Printed and bound in Singapore
10 9 8 7 6 5 4 3 2 1

To my parents, Tom and Dawn, and my brother, Paul. Thank you for always believing in me.

Contents

Introduction

Have you ever wondered why we ask a tongue-tied person, "What's the matter, cat got your tongue?" Or why an extraordinarily unlikely tale is called a "cock-and-bull story"? What does it really mean when we say, "I heard it straight from the horse's mouth"? Animal lovers, take note: countless everyday phrases took their inspirations from our furry, feathered, and scaled friends.

So, where did these expressions come from? With a little digging, we can discover the history behind these familiar phrases. They originated in countries across the world, and from many different cultures and time periods. Although not all expressions can be definitively explained, there's usually at least a good theory or two.

It's Raining Cats and Dogs

Meaning: A torrential downpour.

Origins: Several theories exist about the origins of this phrase. One from seventeenth-century England suggests that heavy rains caused flooding and, sadly, carried the floating bodies of dead dogs and cats along the streets. Another theory links this expression to mythology and superstition; in these stories, cats had influence over the weather. Perhaps this connection came from a superstitious belief that witches, who rode the wind, sometimes took the form of cats. Dogs were attendants of Odin, the storm god, so sailors used to associate these animals with storms.

The Hair of the Dog That Bit You

Meaning: A pick-me-up alcoholic beverage you down the morning after an indulgent night of drinking.

Origins: This saying has its roots in an ancient Roman medical belief: like is cured by like (*similia similibus curantur*). It was a common practice to treat the wound of a dog-bite victim by tying a hair from the dog to the wound with the hope that it would more quickly cure the injury. Similarly, people came to think that the best cure for a hangover would be a bit of the "poison"—alcohol—that caused the condition in the first place.

Go to the Dogs

Meaning: To fall into disrepair, or to otherwise deteriorate in quality.

Origins: Long before dogs became the clean and coddled creatures who now share our beds and homes, they were working dogs. They were kept mainly outdoors—and they certainly were neither clean nor coddled. Often, dinner for a pack of these scraggly dogs consisted of discarded food scraps no longer fit for human consumption. You could say this inferior food had "gone to the dogs."

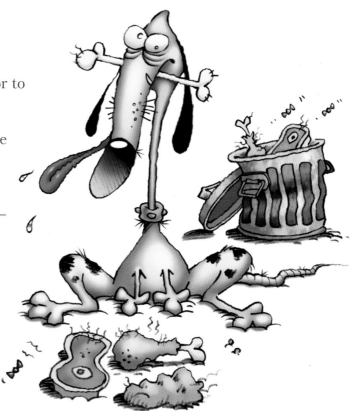

Bark Up the Wrong Tree

Meaning: To be off course, or to search for something in the wrong place.

Origins: This saying most likely originated in America. During hunting excursions, coonhounds chase a raccoon up a tree. The dogs remain at the base of the tree barking and baying until the hunter catches up to shoot the raccoon. Sometimes, especially during night hunts, a raccoon stealthily crawls along the branches and escapes to the safety of a different tree, leaving the dogs literally barking up the wrong tree.

It's Best to Let Sleeping Dogs Lie

Meaning: It's best to leave well enough alone.

Origins: Researchers think this proverbial saying originated in the fourteenth century with Geoffrey Chaucer's *Troilus and Criseyde* (1374): "It is nought good a slepyng hound to wake."

The Dog Days of Summer

Meaning: The hottest time of the year, usually July through August.

Origins: The origin of this saying is quite simple: The ancient Romans believed the intense heat during these summer months came when Sirius, the dog star, rose in the sky at the same time as the sun. Greek myth explains that Sirius is the brightest star in the sky and part of the constellation Canis Major (also called The Greater Dog, one of Orion's canine hunting companions).

Playing Cat and Mouse

Meaning: To tease or fool someone, or to string him along.

Origins: This saying was influenced by the peculiar way cats have of playing with their prey for a while before delivering the final blow. Interestingly, the expression became popular in 1913 in England during the women's suffrage movement. Suffragettes went on hunger strikes to protest their imprisonment. The British government responded with passage of an act that allowed hunger-striking prisoners to be temporarily released for ill health. The catch was that the suffragettes were rearrested once they started eating again and their health was out of danger. Critics dubbed the law the "Cat and Mouse Act" and compared the government to a fat cat cruelly playing with a mouse.

What's the Matter, Cat Got Your Tongue?

Meaning: What's wrong, you don't have an answer? You'd ask this of someone who isn't answering a difficult question, or of someone who is speechless.

Origins: A few theories of the origins of this phrase exist; the following are the most common. Some people believe this expression was influenced by an old Middle Eastern custom of cutting out the tongue of a liar. The severed tongues, as the story goes, were fed to stray cats or to royal pets. Another theory comes from the traditional punishment for sailors—a lashing from a cat-o'-nine-tails. A sailor afraid of getting punished by the "cat" might stay quiet when being reprimanded to avoid a lashing.

Let the Cat Out of the Bag

Meaning: To reveal a secret or disclose information—usually in a surprising manner.

Origins: The most accepted theory of this saying's origins is that it was an old scam. Centuries ago at English country fairs, merchants sold piglets in burlap sacks. Swindlers took advantage of unsuspecting buyers by swapping the piglet for a cat, hoping the buyer wouldn't ask to look in the bag, which of course would let the cat out of the bag and reveal the ruse.

The Cat's Meow

Meaning: Great; the best.

Origins: This American expression became popular in the 1920s as slang for "outstanding." A popular belief credits illustrator Thomas A. Dorgan for coining this expression as well as other similar animal phrases that first appeared in his syndicated cartoons in newspapers across the United States.

Curiosity Killed the Cat

Meaning: Being too inquisitive can be dangerous. Often used as a warning, this phrase advises that curiosity sometimes leads to carelessness and injury.

Origins: Instinctual curiosity makes cats prone to getting into sticky situations. (Has your cat ever followed an exceptionally feisty squirrel up a tree only to become trapped in the highest branches?) Any cat owner can attest that a feline has a tendency to slink around the house and poke her nose into closets, clothes hampers, and trash cans. Whether she eats something she shouldn't or gets trapped somewhere you thought she couldn't, this natural curiosity often gets a nosy kitty into trouble.

Hold Your Horses!

Meaning: Be patient; wait.

Origins: The origins of this phrase can be traced back to nineteenth-century American county fairs. Harness racing (a form of racing in which the horse pulls a light cart and rider at a trot, rather than a gallop) was popular, but the races were sometimes difficult to get underway because the drivers, often inexperienced, would allow their horses to break early, causing the starter to exclaim, "Hold your horses!"

Don't Look a Gift Horse in the Mouth

Meaning: Be gracious when accepting a gift; don't question its value or cost.

Origins: You can estimate the age of a horse by examining its teeth, although it is considered poor manners to look into the mouth of a horse that's been given to you. This saying is so old that its exact origins can't be traced; the earliest recorded use is around AD 400. Variations of this phrase occur in many languages, including Spanish, German, Italian, and French.

On One's High Horse

Meaning: To act arrogantly. Someone who considers himself to be of great importance; someone who acts in a superior manner.

Origins: In Medieval England, people of high rank participating in royal pageants rode atop the best horses used in battle. These horses were generally taller than the other horses and thus referred to as "high horses."

Charley Horse

Meaning: A muscle cramp, especially of the upper leg.

Origins: The most popular explanation of this phrase's origin isn't backed by much evidence, but it's interesting nonetheless. According to one story from the 1890s, a horse named Charley pulled a roller across the infield of the Chicago White Sox ballpark. The baseball fans noticed the horse walked with a limp and soon began to use the phrase, Charley horse, to describe limping ball players.

Pony Up

Meaning: Pay up.

Origins: The popular poker term *pony up* was first used in nineteenth-century America. It may have been derived from the British custom of calling a small amount of money "pony."

Flog (Beat) a Dead Horse

Meaning: To keep a discussion going long after the issue is closed; to waste energy on a fruitless undertaking.

Origins: This meaning of this phrase, recorded as early as the seventeenth century, is quite obvious (not to mention morbid). If a horse is dead, attempting to compel it to pull a cart by flogging it is entirely useless. The French have a similar—and equally disturbing— phrase, *chercher à ressusciter un mort*, which means, "to seek to resurrect a corpse."

SACRE BLEU...
DUNT POOP OUT
on me now!

Wild Goose Chase

Meaning: Foolish pursuit of something unlikely to be caught.

Origins: Englishmen in the late sixteenth century invented a game played on horseback called a wild goose chase, in which the lead horse ran off in any direction, and the rest of the horses had to follow—no matter how erratic the course. From a distance, the formation resembled a flock of geese in flight. The earliest use of the phrase simply meant an unpredictable route chosen by one person and followed by another. Over time, the phrase evolved to mean a fruitless endeavor.

As the Crow Flies

Meaning: In as straight and direct a path as possible.

Origins: This phrase is straightforward: a crow in flight will take the most direct route and wouldn't need to traverse around streams, lakes, and hills. The earliest recorded version of this phrase appeared in 1800, used then as "the crow's road."

A Little Bird Told Me

Meaning: I received the information from a secret or private source.

Origins: Although etymologists do not agree on this expression's origins, a common explanation is that this phrase was born of a biblical passage (Ecclesiastes 10:20): "Curse not the king, no not in thy thought; and curse not the rich in thy bedchamber: for a bird of the air shall carry the voice, and that which hath wings shall tell the matter."

Don't Count Your Chickens Before They're Hatched

Meaning: Don't rely on future profits until you actually have them.

Origins: Arguably, this phrase may have been influenced by a story in *Aesop's Fables*. In "The Milkmaid and Her Pail," a woman takes her eggs to sell at the market. She claims she'll buy a goose with the money from the eggs, and a cow with the profits from her goose, and so on, her excitement growing as she dreams of her coming fortune. Alas, in her eagerness to get to the market, the woman kicks over her bucket and breaks the eggs—dashing her hopes of profit.

The Early Bird Catches the Worm

Meaning: Whoever arrives first has the best chance at the reward.

Origins: British author William Camden (1551–1623) is credited with coining this expression. It holds the same meaning today: just as the first bird to see the worm gets the prize, a person who's first to seize an opportunity reaps the reward.

She's No Spring Chicken

Meaning: She is past her prime.

Origins: The original version of this saying, "now past a chicken," appeared in 1711 in an English periodical, *The Spectator*. A spring chicken, in a literal sense, is a young bird with tender meat ready for eating. The expression took its figurative form in the United States in the early 1900s as a way to describe a lady who's in her prime. You could of course use it conversely—she's no spring chicken—to indicate a woman who's lost her youthful appearance.

Till the Cows Come Home

Meaning: A very long time.

Origins: This seventeenth-century phrase gets its meaning from cows' tendency to stay out in the pasture for a long period of time unless rounded up by the farmer. Cows need to be milked twice a day, and if a farmer waits too long, the cows' udders become swollen with milk, which is quite painful. Although cows will stay out overnight if allowed, they'll find their way home on their own when it's milking time!

Going the Whole Hog

Meaning: Doing something wholeheartedly, completely; going all the way.

Origins: One popular theory is that in the early nineteenth century, a "hog" was slang in the United States for a ten-cent piece. Someone willing to spend an entire ten cents would be spending the whole hog, or going all out.

Living High on the Hog

Meaning: Living very well. This phrase can refer to an affluent person's high-end lifestyle or to simply indicate someone is well fed (which implies that he can afford to eat rich food—and plenty of it).

Origins: This saying was born of well-to-do, meat-eating folks. The superior, most-expensive cuts of pork are taken from the upper parts of the hog.

Scapegoat

Meaning: A person—usually innocent or only one of many culprits—who is blamed for wrongdoings.

Origins: This term comes from an Old Testament Bible passage in which a priest lays all the sins of the people on a goat and then sends the goat out into the woods. The *scape* part of the word most likely comes from a mistranslation on the part of William Tyndale (c. 1492–1536), who mistook the Hebrew word *'azazel*, the name of a demon, as *'ez ozel*, the goat that departs.

Get One's Goat

Meaning: To irritate, annoy, or anger someone.

Origins: One colorful theory links this expression to horse racing. Thoroughbreds sometimes have goats as stable mates because the goats seem to have a calming effect on the horses. Horses are creatures of habit and become attached to their goat friends. If the goat were stolen the night before a big race, the horse might be expected to do poorly at the race. Getting the goat of a horse who is expected to win could mean big money for gamblers.

Take the Bull by the Horns

Meaning: To confront a difficult issue or situation head-on.

Origins: The most likely origin of this phrase is the Spanish sport of bullfighting. The matadors weaken the bull by spearing it in the neck with darts. They then seize the bull by its horns in an effort to bring its nose to the ground.

A Cock-and-Bull Story

Meaning: An imaginative, but ultimately unlikely tale.

Origins: Most likely, this phrase originated from a fable about a cock and a bull, in which the two animals spoke to each other in human language; however, it's never been traced to an exact story or author.

In a Pig's Eye

Meaning: Never, or it's a lie.

Origins: One theory suggests that *pig's eye* rhymes with *lie*, so, this expression is a cryptic way of saying the person is lying.

Go Hog Wild

Meaning: To become wildly excited, enthusiastic—even irrational.

Origins: This farm phrase originated in nineteenth-century America. It refers to the way that hogs become extremely excited when stimulated, such as at feeding time.

Like a Bat Out of Hell

Meaning: Moving very fast. "She ran out of the building like a bat out of hell."

Origins: Although the exact origin is unknown, this phrase has been traced to the early 1900s and was used by British pilots in World War I as slang for flying very fast. It's a fact of nature that bats are nocturnal and avoid light. So, they would fly extremely fast to get away from the bright flames of hell.

Playing Possum

Meaning: To pretend, or to deceive. Playing possum means pretending to be dead with the hope that an approaching predator will pass you by.

Origins: This expression originated in the United States when early Americans discovered the strange-looking possum and its interesting way of feigning death in order to avoid being caught.

The Straw That Broke the Camel's Back

Meaning: The final breaking point.

Origins: Camels are extremely strong—they can carry as much as one thousand pounds on their backs. Charles Dickens used this expression in his novel *Dombey and Son* (1847–1848): "As the last straw breaks the laden camel's back." However, an old English proverb was around long before Dickens' novel: "'Tis the last feather that breaks the horse's back."

Clam Up

Meaning: To become quiet, or to refuse to disclose information.

Origins: This American saying, commonly used since the nineteenth century, refers to the difficulty of prying open the two "lips" of a clam shell.

Happy as a Clam

Meaning: Very happy, secure.

Origins: The original version of this saying reveals its meaning more easily: happy as a clam at high tide. Clams are usually dug at low tide, when they are exposed. The water level at high tide conceals the clams in their sandy beds, making it difficult for someone to pluck them from their homes. Thus, we could assume that a clam would feel quite secure and happy at high tide.

The Lion's Share

Meaning: The biggest portion of something.

Origins: This expression comes from a version of a story in *Aesop's Fables*. In it, a lion, an ass, and a fox catch a stag while on a hunting trip. Trying his best to be fair, the ass divides the meal into three equal portions. The lion believes his size, ability, and dignity are deserving of a larger portion. Enraged, he kills the ass.
With the ass dead, it's up to the fox to divide the meal. Wishing to stay alive, the crafty fox takes a tiny piece for himself and leaves the rest of the share to the lion.

Poor as a Church Mouse

Meaning: Extremely poor.

Origins: This expression dates back to seventeenth-century England; the German and French have similar sayings. In those days, a church was basically a simple place in which to pray or to go for confession. Churches did not have multipurpose halls to host post–Sunday service luncheons or have kitchen pantries with food for the needy. A mouse who took up residence in a seventeenth-century church rarely could find a crumb to nibble. Thus, *poor as a church mouse* describes the destitute.

A Frog in One's Throat

Meaning: To be hoarse, or to have lost your voice.

Origins: Some researchers think this phrase came about simply because of the croaking sound a person with a hoarse voice makes. Others contend that it was born of an old wives' tale that claimed if you drank from a pond you could swallow a tadpole that would grow into a frog in your throat.

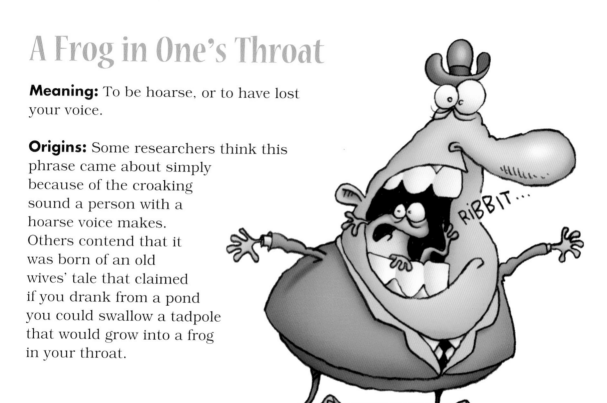

RIBBIT...

A Snake in the Grass

Meaning: A sneaky, deceitful person who pretends to be a friend to someone he actually intends to harm or to take advantage of. It is a metaphor for treachery.

Origins: This phrase first appeared in the Roman poet Virgil's *Third Eclogue*: "Latet anguis in herba" (a snake lurks in the grass).

Eager Beaver

Meaning: Raring to go; ready for whatever may come. We often use this to describe a person with a strong work ethic, as in, "That boy's an eager beaver!"

Origins: This Canadian army expression was first recorded in 1940. It refers to the industrious beaver who never ceases his work building river dams.

Opening a Can of Worms

Meaning: To initiate or provoke discussion on a touchy topic; to open the figurative door to a situation in which you're bound to find trouble.

Origins: This phrase was first recorded in the United States during the mid-twentieth century. It refers to opening a can of food only to find worms inside. Some researchers specifically attribute the phrase to fishermen keeping live bait in small jars or cans.

About the Author

Jackie Franza received her bachelor of arts degree from the University of California, Irvine. She is the editor of multiple dog and cat magazines, including *Dogs USA* and *Cats USA*, and has published several articles in pet-related magazines. She's based in Southern California, where she enjoys racing Hawaiian-style outrigger canoes in the beautiful Pacific Ocean. She shares her home with her cat, Sebastian.

Resources

Books

Knowles, Elizabeth, ed. *The Oxford Dictionary of Phrase and Fable.* New York: Oxford University Press, 2000.

Hendrickson, Robert. *The Facts on File Encyclopedia of Word and Phrase Origins.* 3rd ed. New York, NY: Facts on File, 2004.

———. *The Facts on File Encyclopedia of Word and Phrase Origins,* rev. ed. New York, NY: Facts on File, 1997.

Room, Adrian, ed. *Brewer's Dictionary of Modern Phrase and Fable.* London: Cassell, 2000.

Funk, Charles E. *Heavens to Betsy! And Other Curious Sayings.* New York: Harper, 1955.

———. *A Hog on Ice and Other Curious Expressions.* New York: Harper, 1948.

Morris, William. *Morris Dictionary of Word and Phrase Origins.* New York: Harper & Row, 1988.

Web Sites

http://www.phrases.org.uk
http://www.wordorigins.org